A Gift for:

From:

What I
Learned from
God Today

SIMPLE TRUTHS TO RENEW
AND STRENGTHEN YOUR FAITH

What I Learned from God Today
Copyright © 2006 by J. Countryman

Published by J. Countryman®, a division of Thomas Nelson Book Group,
Nashville, Tennessee 37214

Unless otherwise noted, Scripture quotations are from the *New King James
Version*, copyright © 1979,1980,1982,1992, Thomas Nelson, Inc.

Other Scripture quotations are from: *The Holy Bible*, New International
Version (NIV) © 1984 by the International Bible Society. Used by permis-
sion of Zondervan Bible Publishers; *King James Version* (KJV); *The Message*
(MSG) © 1993. Used by permission of NavPress Publishing Group; *The
Holy Bible*, New Living Translation (NLT), © 1996. Used by permission of
Tyndale House Publishers, Inc., Wheaton, Illinois. All rights reserved; *New
Life Version* (NLV) © 1969 by Christian Living International (CLI).

Project Manager: Lisa Stilwell
Project Editor: Pat Matuszak

Designed by The DesignWorks Group, www.thedesignworksgroup.com

ISBN 978-1-4041-0379-5

www.jcountryman.com / www.thomasnelson.com

Printed in China

Table of Contents

The Dehydrated Heart

Jesus stood and cried out, saying,
"If anyone thirsts, let him come to Me and drink.
He who believes in Me, as the Scripture
has said, out of his heart will flow rivers of living water."

JOHN 7:37–38

S top drinking [water] and see what happens. Coherent thoughts vanish, skin grows clammy, and vital organs wrinkle. Your Maker wired you with thirst—a "low-fluid indicator." Deprive your body of necessary fluid, and it will tell you.

Deprive your soul of spiritual water, and your soul will tell you. Dehydrated hearts send desperate messages. Snarling tempers. Waves of worry. Hopelessness. Sleeplessness. Loneliness. Resentment. These are warnings symptoms of a dryness deep within.

Don't you need regular sips from God's reservoir? I do. I've offered this prayer in countless situations; stressful meetings, dull days, long drives, demanding trips, character-testing decisions. Many times a day I step to the underground spring of God and receive anew his work for my sin and death, the energy of his Spirit, his lordship, and his love.

MAX LUCADO, *Come Thirsty*

Toward this end, I give you this tool: a prayer for the thirsty heart.

It outlines four essential fluids for soul hydration: God's work, God's energy, his lordship, and his love. Just think of the word *W-E-L-L.*

> Lord, I come thirsty. I come to drink, to receive. I receive your Work on the cross and in your resurrection. My sins are pardoned, and my death is defeated. I receive your Energy. Empowered by your Holy Spirit, I can do all things through Christ, who gives me strength. I receive your Lordship. I belong to you. Nothing comes to me that hasn't passed through you. And I receive your Love. Nothing can separate me from your love.

WHAT I LEARNED FROM GOD TODAY...

Epiphanies

You will keep him in perfect peace,
Whose mind is stayed on You,
Because he trusts in You.

ISAIAH 26:3

E piphanies are sudden, intuitive perceptions or insights.
I've come to recognize them as symbolic revelations from
God. One such moment of truth happened when I realized
my life had greater meaning than the choices I'd been making.
I began to see that choices are sacred. God created us and gives
us the opportunities to make choices. This means that we can
become co-creators with God in deciding our future. I've come
to understand that there is an invisible, spiritual world. As we
make inspired conscious choices, we're opening up to infinite
possibilities. God is always there, invisible but all-knowing and
available for us to turn to.

When it comes time to make a choice, realizing what we
don't want can help us see what we do want to do. My
epiphany caused me to look back on my choices with newly
informed eyes. I immediately became clear about what I
didn't want anymore. I didn't like the way I'd been raising
Wy and Ashley and I no longer wanted any part of the over-
stimulated, materialistic, phony Hollywood lifestyle.

LIVING OUT GOD'S PLAN FOR MY LIFE

What was important to me was Wy and Ash knowing their heritage and being close to our family. I also wanted time and opportunity to tune in to them. Once I became aware of the huge discrepancy between the choices I'd been making and my true values, I began the necessary steps toward bringing my life into alignment with my values.

NAOMI JUDD, *The Transparent Life*

WHAT I LEARNED FROM GOD TODAY...

Everyone Wants
to Know the Secret

Pray to your Father who is in the secret place;
and your Father who sees in secret will reward you openly.

MATTHEW 6:6

E veryone wants to know the secret to something.
Golfers want to know the secret to playing golf like
Tiger Woods. Investors want to know the secret to making a
fortune on Wall Street. Parents want to know the secret to
raising healthy, happy kids. And Christians desperately want
to know the secrets to effective prayer. So, what are the secrets
to real intimacy with God?

The first secret to effective prayer is secret prayer. And
Jesus provided the ultimate example. As Dr. Luke puts it, he
"often withdrew to lonely places and prayed" (Luke 5:16, NIV).
Unlike the religious leaders of his day, Jesus did not pray to
be seen by men. He prayed because he treasured fellowship
with his Father. Hypocrites gain their reward through public
prayer. They may be perceived as spiritual giants, but by the
time they are finished, they have received everything they
will ever get—their prayer's worth and nothing more.

A further secret is to recognize the connection between
prayer and meditation. Our prayers are only as inspired as
our intake of Scripture. Meditation on Scripture allows us to

more naturally transition into a marvelous time of meaningful prayer.

A final secret is to discover your secret place, a place where you can drown out the static of the world and hear the voice of your Heavenly Father.

LIVING OUT GOD'S PLAN FOR MY LIFE

Your secret place will no doubt be different than mine. The point is that we all desperately need a place away from the invasive sounds of this world so that we can hear the sounds of another place and another Voice.

HANK HANEGRAAFF, *The Bible Answer Book*

WHAT I LEARNED FROM GOD TODAY...

God Listens

Everything GOD does is right—
the trademark on all his works is love.

PSALM 145:17, THE MESSAGE

God not only speaks to us, he listens to us. His listening to us is an even greater marvel than his speaking to us. We cannot define God; we cannot package God. But that doesn't mean that we are completely at sea with God, never knowing what to expect, nervously on edge all the time, wondering what he might do. We know very well what to expect, and what we expect is mercy.

We need not muddle through half the day, or half our lives, before God shows up, rubbing his eyes, asking if there is anything he might do for us.

He knows the kind of world we live in and our vulnerability to it. He is there right on time to help.

LIVING OUT GOD'S PLAN FOR MY LIFE
The loving-kindness of the Lord is given
to the people of all times who honor Him.

LUKE 1:50, NLV

EUGENE H. PETERSON, *A Message of Comfort and Hope*

WHAT I LEARNED FROM GOD TODAY...

What If?

For we are His workmanship,
created in Christ Jesus for good works,
which God prepared beforehand
that we should walk in them.

EPHESIANS 2:10

We can revel in the promises of God about Christ's return and reign and about the new heaven and the new earth. We love to read the last chapters of Revelation, but we get hung up on our immediate problems. The problems of war, disease, famine, the plague of AIDS, and weapons of mass destruction blur the vision of the ultimate reign and rule of the King of Kings and the Prince of Peace. Many times, our theology about the immutable works of God crumbles in the face of "What if?"

Yet God is gracious to us—as He was to Moses. He said, "All right, I'll deal with the 'What ifs.' What do you have in your hand?" Moses said, "A staff." This was a rod about six feet long. It was a walking pole. He leaned on that staff to get a little rest, or he used it as a weapon to defend the flock he was shepherding. But the rod was more than a tool; it was also a symbol of power and authority, a sign of a person's tribe and identity. In fact, the word *rod* in the Old Testament means "tribe" in over 250 references. Every tribe had a rod.

So God told Moses, "Throw it down." Moses obeyed, and instantly the rod became a snake. It was a miracle of God and a demonstration of His power.

LIVING OUT GOD'S PLAN FOR MY LIFE

You have a rod in your hand, a ruling authority in your life. Are you going to keep your hand grasped tightly on it, ruling your own life, or will you throw it down in faith? Will you let God rule in—and guide—you?

FRANKLIN GRAHAM WITH ROSS RHOADS, *All for Jesus*

WHAT I LEARNED FROM GOD TODAY...

A Place to Heal

He has delivered us from the power of darkness
and conveyed us into the kingdom of the Son of His love.

COLOSSIANS 1:13

Years ago, when I was a divorced mother of two little
girls looking for a church home, I went from church to
church, desperately seeking a place where I could grow in
Christ and get my life back on track. Thankfully, the Lord
led me to that place, and that was the beginning of my
healing . . . and my journey back to God.

Some time later, as my pastor spoke to the congregation
about our mission to help hurting people, he said that
Christians too often shoot their wounded. He said that our
church's mission was "to send an ambulance instead of a
firing squad." And that's just what the church did for me,
through people who'd experienced what I was suffering, and
others who used their God-given gifts to minister to me in
my time of need.

But I don't see that working in every church, nor do I
see it working in my own all the time. Too often, I see 5
percent of the congregation doing a 100 percent of the
work. The other 95 percent just want to be fed. They sit in
their pews Sunday after Sunday, like the man-eating plant
in "Little Shop of Horrors," crying, "Feed Me, Seymour!"

And the workers do everything they can to accommodate.

LIVING OUT GOD'S PLAN FOR MY LIFE

What could happen if we each used our gifts as God intended? How would it change us to see God working through those gifts, using every part of the body of Christ, to minister to a hurting world?

TERRI BLACKSTOCK, *The Gifted*

WHAT I LEARNED FROM GOD TODAY...

_____

_____

_____

_____

_____

_____

_____

_____

_____

_____

The Cross Is Not in the Cellar

*But God forbid that I should boast except
in the cross of our Lord Jesus Christ . . .
And as many as walk according to this rule,
peace and mercy be upon them . . . ."*

GALATIANS 6:14, 16

I began to see a counselor to help me work through the tangled web of what I was feeling.

"You tell me to stop losing it, but what do I do with everything I feel?" I asked. "I don't want to go back to living in a glass house while my emotions live in the cellar. I want all of me to be in the same room!"

He laughed at my convoluted analogy.

"That's what God wants for you, too."

What I have discovered as I have prayed and studied and asked God for His wisdom is this, it is very simple but to me profound:

You no longer have to take your stuff to the cellar; you can take it to the cross.

What a life-changing truth!

Living out God's Plan for My Life

I am not an advocate of the quick fix, and this journey has been no exception, but I have to tell you that since I began living like this I feel as if I have been let out of a cage. I am learning by God's grace to take a few moments out when I feel the overwhelming urge to respond in anger or out of fear or insecurity. I'll find a quiet spot (usually the restroom!) and talk through my feelings with my Father. Once I have dumped all my stuff on Him I am able to pick up only what's appropriate to share with whomever I might have a difference. I want to speak words of kindness and encouragement, not dissention and hurt.

SHEILA WALSH, *Come As You Are*

What I Learned from God Today...

_____

_____

_____

_____

_____

_____

_____

Sin Is the Monster
We Love to Deny

"Come now, and let us reason together," says the LORD.
"Though your sins are like scarlet,
they shall be as white as snow...."

ISAIAH 1:18

I t can stalk us, bite a slice out of our lives, return again and bite again, and even as we bleed and hobble, we prefer to believe nothing has happened. It makes sin the perfect monster, a man-eater that blinds and numbs its victims, convincing them that nothing is wrong and there is no need to flee, and then consumes them at its leisure.

We've all been assailed by this beast, sometimes face-to-face, but all too often from a direction we aren't prepared to defend, and it's only in recognizing the beast for what it is that we can hope to escape at all. In Jesus Christ we are forgiven and empowered to overcome sin, but opening the door and tossing the beast kitchen scraps of our character is no way to drive it off. Toying with an animal that is actually toying with us is a sure way to lose part of ourselves.

I was watching it happen to some friends of mine the year I began writing *The Oath*. As the rest of us just kept on praising the Lord, loving one another, smiling, and trying not to be judgmental, some really good people walked stupidly, blindly into the jaws of sin. The tooth marks still show today, in ruined marriages and soiled ministries. The rest of us should have said something.

FRANK PERETTI, The Oath

LIVING OUT GOD'S PLAN FOR MY LIFE
How can you strengthen your friends and love them both honestly and courageously?

WHAT I LEARNED FROM GOD TODAY...

Walk into Your Future

*For God so loved the world
that He gave His only begotten Son,
that whoever believes in Him should not perish
but have everlasting life.*

John 3:16

God's Word tells us that we become new creatures the moment we accept Jesus as our Savior. That doesn't mean we instantly experience a new environment, new circumstances, new situations, or new relationships. There's a walking out and a working out that's our responsibility. We are the ones who have to create and establish a new atmosphere for our lives—an atmosphere that is focused on God and based on His Word.

We are the ones who need to develop new circumstances and new situations that are good in God's eyes. We are the ones who need to form new relationships that are godly, encouraging, and beneficial.

Living out God's Plan for My Life

If you continue to look back, you won't be qualified to possess what God has for you. Look ahead, not back. Don't look to what might have been, should have been, or could have been! Look at what is to be!

PAULA WHITE, *A Sensational Life*

What I Learned from God Today...

His Presence Is Sure

"Your Father knows exactly what you need, before you ask Him!"

MATTHEW 6:8, NLT

I've lived alone for the past twelve years. If somebody had told me a decade ago that I could do it, I'd have said, "No way." And yet today I have the most awesome sense of peace and happiness and joy in my heart because I know I'm never really alone. There was a time when walking into my empty home bothered me, but after a while the Lord reminded me that He is always with me. I think of how much more time I have these days to spend with Him. He turned what, at first, was my complaint into a real comfort. I know now that He is adequate and that He will turn the lonely hours into a fruitful time in my life. In fact, He's already done that.

There is no substitute for personal intimacy with God. Nothing compares with it—it is the key to everything.

LIVING OUT GOD'S PLAN FOR MY LIFE

Most people are looking for an exciting and fulfilling life, and they're looking in all the wrong places: money, prestige, and relationships—mostly relationships. They are looking for something that they can achieve to bring about fulfillment, or someone they can meet who will make their small life grow. But there isn't anything we can do or anyone we can meet who will sufficiently fill the void in our hearts. As Thomas Aquinas said, "There is a God-shaped void in all of us." The only thing that can fill the indescribably longing within each human heart is God's presence. The gift of His Son abiding in us is totally adequate for everything we do.

DR. CHARLES STANLEY, *Living the Extraordinary Life*

WHAT I LEARNED FROM GOD TODAY...

The Gift of Plod

Let us lay aside every weight,
and the sin which so easily ensnares us,
and let us run with endurance the race that is set before us,
looking unto Jesus, the author and finisher of our faith....

HEBREWS 12:1–2

We named our calico kitty Nara, short for *naranja*, the Spanish word for orange. Timing is not Nara's forte. But she knows she was born to catch birds, so every day she crouches and waits and pounces, unsuccessfully, only to crouch and wait and pounce again. It matters not that she has failed miserably at ALL attempts to catch a bird EVERY day of her life. She will wake up tomorrow and try again. Nara has the gift of *plod*.

Reminds me of Abraham Lincoln who lost how many elections on his road to winning one—the presidency I believe? Or William Carey, missionary to India, who waited seven years before he saw one person decide to follow Christ.

Why didn't they give up? Perhaps this unglamorous gift of plod is worth more than we imagine.

LIVING OUT GOD'S PLAN FOR MY LIFE

The Lincolns and Careys of this world choose . . .

to equate an unsuccessful attempt with a lesson learned;

to believe that obedience walks under the banner of effort, not ease;

to trust God more than they fear failure.

And with each choice, they plod on to change the world.

ALICIA BRITT CHOLE, *Pure Joy!*

WHAT I LEARNED FROM GOD TODAY . . .

Midnight Journal

"LORD, You will establish peace for us. . . ."
ISAIAH 26:12

During college, I used to do a lot of my journaling at the coffee shop, writing about my struggle to know and love God, and my problems with myself or with the opposite sex.

The journaling about relationships with men was usually dramatic and tragically toned! I thought God had barred me from finding a happy relationship with a man because I wanted it so badly. It never crossed my mind he was simply answering my childhood prayers that I would only love one man. Because I had forgotten those prayers, I felt forgotten by the One in whom I had placed my deepest trust. But as it turned out I wasn't cursed, just impatient, ungrateful, and forgetful—like the Hebrews in the wilderness, whining even after God parted the Red Sea and sent manna from heaven. They constantly doubted God's ability to take care of them! But I'm no different because, now that I am happily married, I still keep asking "Now what?" God answered my deepest wishes and I'm already worrying about what will happen next!

Living out God's Plan for My Life

The "now whats" keep me awake, not my beautiful husband's snoring or the coffee I drank at 7 p.m. It's the anxiety of not being able to see what cards God is holding to deal me next. Will my life turn out the way I'm planning? What if it doesn't? I think it is wise to view anxiousness as a temptation to sin. Seriously. Not trusting God must be considered an insult to Him after everything He has promised and fulfilled! Most likely, my life won't turn out exactly as I've planned—it will be better! If I can learn to trust the One who is most deserving of my trust, I might even have fun on the journey.

CHRISTI BISSELL, www.EditorialCoffee.com

What I Learned from God Today...

31

He Is Always Near

Draw near to God and He will draw near to you.

JAMES 4:8

None of us wants to be "left." And yet we all are left at some point in our lives. I wish it weren't true. Someone leaves—whether through a deliberate act of walking out the door or the devastating passage of death—it happens. It is part of living here and enduring mortal bodies and possessing selfish hearts.

We were all built for relationship—first and foremost with our Creator, who in turn blessed us with the desire for relationship. There is a yearning in all of us to love and be loved. There is a longing to know and be known.

LIVING OUT GOD'S PLAN FOR MY LIFE

Sometimes you may know someone who will do something that is contrary to what you have experienced from them. You might say, "That was so out of character for him." We can never say that about Jesus. He is consistent and unconditional in his wisdom and his love. You can count on it. He is the house you come home to after a long trip. It's safe and secure. It's a haven and a hiding place. That is so reassuring to me. It brings me such comfort, especially being single and now without parents.

KATHY TROCCOLI, *A Love That Won't Walk Away*

What I Learned from God Today...

A New Beginning

You turned for me my mourning into dancing; You have put off my sackcloth and clothed me with gladness, to the end that my glory may sing praise to You and not be silent. O LORD my God, I will give thanks to You forever.

PSALM 30:11–12

After sixteen years of marriage, I was devastated when it ended in divorce, and I was scared wondering what I was going to do to support myself and two children. I hadn't worked full-time in twelve years. I wasn't overly enthusiastic about job hunting and I didn't like the idea of leaving my kids to get off to school by themselves. Concentrating on work would be difficult, because my mind would reflect back on my personal situation. When it did the tears would flow. I prayed, asking the Lord to help me find a job that I could handle. A dear uncle of mine came to see me. He had a lot of connections and thought he might be able to help me get a job. We went to see two of his business acquaintances and left an application with each. Neither one had any openings, but they said they would keep me in mind. After a couple of weeks and no job offers I decided maybe I should put in an application myself.

I took my application to one business and found the lady I needed to speak with wasn't in, so I just left my information for her. The next morning she called and asked me to come in for an interview. I walked out of her office knowing that the Lord had answered my prayer abundantly! He had even worked out the cares of my heart. Not only did I get an interesting job, but I was able to come in an hour later, so I was at home to send my children off to school each day.

After growing through this experience, I knew the Lord was showing me that I could rely on Him to work things out for me right down to the smallest detail, and I have often reminded myself of what He taught me through troubles.

LIVING OUT GOD'S PLAN FOR MY LIFE

How has God shown His faithfulness to you in the past? How is the Holy Spirit reminding you of His love today?

BRENDA BOWAN, www.EditorialCoffee.com

WHAT I LEARNED FROM GOD TODAY...

Worth the Risk

And we know that all things work together
for good to those who love God,
to those who are the called according to His purpose.

ROMANS 8:28

Life without risk is not much of a life. I know young men who inherited a lot of money and had all the comforts and securities you could possibly ask for. They had it all but lived with no fire in the belly because there was nothing to burn. Because their lives were so predictable and comfortable and risk free, they missed becoming the men they could have been.

Predictability really can chain us to old things and prevent us from moving toward the new. Comfort can encase us in a womb we should have outgrown but still retreat into. We must give up the chains of predictability and the womb of comfort and jump out there and take a risk if we are to truly live.

Risk is a choice to heal because it stretches some of the scar tissue and prevents us from being restrained by the energy. Just like a burn patient who must painfully move the scarred limbs to stretch the skin, we must do the same with our souls. We must stretch into what is not comfortable, so that we do not confine ourselves to what is comfortable. That stretching comes from risk.

LIVING OUT GOD'S PLAN FOR MY LIFE

We risk connecting, because if we don't, parts of us will die in isolation. We must risk loving again, because if we don't, we will become bitter and isolated. We risk succeeding, knowing that it might prove to be a failure and we might look inadequate. If we do not risk, however, we will live a horrible life of boredom and loneliness, convincing ourselves we are okay as we mark time toward a miserable end. It does not have to be that way if we will choose to take a risk.

STEVE ARTERBURN, *Healing Is a Choice Devotional*

WHAT I LEARNED FROM GOD TODAY...

Grace Over Time

*For all who have sinned and fall short
of the glory of God, being justified freely by His grace
through the redemption that is in Christ Jesus.*

ROMANS 3:23–24

Twenty-four years had elapsed since that blustery November day when I had given up my first child. By this time I was a mother of four, and my marriage of twenty-one years was faltering under the pressure of many stresses.

I heard God's voice when I was invited to a local pregnancy care center. It was there that I learned more about the healing work offered for people like me suffering from post-abortive stress syndrome. I knew the anguish I felt was real. I just didn't know it was a recognized disorder. I never expected that a Christian organization would respond to my pain with love and support. Because of their loving spirit, I learned about a merciful and gracious God, who had abounding love for me, could heal me, and also use my experience to provide healing and comfort to others. And it was then that I realized that God had forgiven me, and had cast away my transgressions, "As far as the east is from the west" (Psalm 103:12).

Living out God's Plan for My Life

For many years, I couldn't understand the purpose of my experiences: crisis pregnancy, pregnancy loss, and becoming an adoptive mother. But these experiences have helped shape me into who I am today, and they have allowed me to see the evidences of God's grace and forgiveness. I have grieved and let go of the shame. And for this I am grateful for a forgiving and merciful God.

KATHY PRIDE, www.tapestryministry.com

What I Learned from God Today...

A Bend in the Road

In You, O LORD, I put my trust....
Be my strong refuge, to which I may resort continually;
You have given the commandment to save me,
for You are my rock and my fortress.

[Recalling his struggle with cancer, Dr. David Jeremiah writes:]

I remember so well the time when I came to my bend in
the road. Everything God had given me to do was growing and thriving. The size of our church had doubled. The
number of listeners to our *Turning Point* nationwide radio
ministry had doubled. The books I had written were finding
larger audiences. People were responding to our ministry.
All of this was for the glory of God. And then, right in the
midst of all these blessings, came the disruptive moment.
On the face of things it seemed to make so little sense.

Have you had that kind of experience? Just when you
had everything lined up in your life exactly as you wanted
things to be, you experienced an unwelcome and unantici-
pated disaster that spoiled everything. And you asked many
questions, all beginning with the word *why*.

"Why this, Lord?" you might ask. "Why now? Why not
later? Why not someone else?"

LIVING OUT GOD'S PLAN FOR MY LIFE

We all ask the "why" questions. They're a natural part of being human. But we can ask better questions—we can ask "what" questions: "What, Lord? What would You have me do? What are You trying to teach me?"

DAVID JEREMIAH, *When Your World Falls Apart*

WHAT I LEARNED FROM GOD TODAY...

_____

_____

_____

_____

_____

_____

_____

_____

_____

_____

_____

_____

Teach Me, Lord

For You, Lord, are good, and ready to forgive,
and abundant in mercy to all those who call upon You.

PSALM 86:5

Fishermen, since the beginning of time, have been asking for help and advice on how to catch more fish. Jesus told Peter where to cast his net, and some of us today make our living telling others how to become better fishermen. I know people who have driven hundreds of miles to listen to a top tournament pro give a seminar. They do this just to be more successful on the water.

God is the ultimate expert, and He is ready and willing to answer our questions and to come to our aid. All we need to do is ask. But somehow—out of "macho-ness," lack of faith, or whatever—we'll not come to God and ask until it's the last resort. If we'll get God involved in today's problems and concerns right now, we'll likely not need to use God as the last resort tomorrow.

LIVING OUT GOD'S PLAN FOR MY LIFE

Lord, I want to come to you first, not last, for expert advice!
Help me to remember that lesson when I start looking
around for an answer.

JIMMY HOUSTON, *Catch of the Day*

WHAT I LEARNED FROM GOD TODAY...

Your Authentic Self

It is the God who commanded light to shine out of darkness,
who has shone in our hearts to give the light of the
knowledge of the glory of God in the face of Jesus Christ.

2 CORINTHIANS 4:6

Sometimes it's helpful to get an outside perspective on how you are doing as a professional—or as a person, a parent, or a friend. Most of us have mentors in life, whether they know it or not, to whom we look for an example or an anchor during choppy emotional waters in our career or personal life. It was during one of those times that I asked for career advice from one of the most discerning mentors I know. This was his short, but stunning, reply: "Just be your authentic self."

Our authentic self springs from our dreams and talents. It is our genuine self that God's heart envisioned when he created us. It's not selfish to nurture our genuine nature, because that's where we will find the resources to bless others. When circumstances or people are locking you into activities that are contrary to the things you know in your heart God is guiding and gifting you toward, seek freedom to follow your authentic path.

LIVING OUT GOD'S PLAN FOR MY LIFE

Our authentic life may follow a completely different path
from the one other people imagine for us. God has put His
light in us so that we can see to walk that path. He fills our
fragile human forms with His light to both illuminate our
own way and shine out of our life for others.

PAT MATUSZAK, www.EditorialCoffee.com

WHAT I LEARNED FROM GOD TODAY...

The Perfect Serve

For to me, to live is Christ, and to die is gain.

PHILIPPIANS 1:21

S erving requires skill and modesty. A servant is seen, but he shouldn't be obvious. He's in the background, he's available, he's always ready, he knows what to do. The servant anticipates what the master wants, like a good waiter does in a fine dining establishment. This is the way Paul served the Lord.

How prone we are to fail in this attitude toward our service for the Lord, even in ministry positions. Some people who haven't been called are in the business of Christianity. They are attracted by the promise of profit or popularity, or by an attractive career choice. A market-driven culture tends to drive spiritual movements, resulting in the loss of a heavenly vision of the call of God. We should feel cautioned and warned that in any ministry, as popular and successful as it may be, we must be sure our ultimate motivation is serving the Lord. Self-service brings God's judgment (1 Samuel 2:25–26).

Service should be wholehearted. Paul said, "In the ministry that the Lord has given to me, I have not held back." It sounds almost arrogant, but it wasn't. "I count not my life dear unto myself," he stated bluntly.

Living out God's Plan for My Life

Later, while in prison, he reiterated this commitment to the Philippians: "For to me, to live is Christ, and to die is gain" (Philippians 1:21). He knew the focal point of ministry was selfless service, even to the point of death for Jesus and the Gospel. "We are not trying to please men but God, who tests our hearts" (1 Thessalonians 2:4, NIV). We have a choice. Are we going to serve ourselves, or are we going to serve the Lord?

FRANKLIN GRAHAM WITH ROSS RHOADS, *All for Jesus*

What I Learned from God Today...

More Than Bread

And Jesus answered and said to her, "Martha, Martha,
you are worried and troubled about many things.
But one thing is needed, and Mary has chosen that good
part, which will not be taken away from her."

LUKE 10:41–42

I've always had company over, but I've not always enjoyed
them. It used to take me a day to prepare, a day to entertain,
and another day just to recover. That changed a few years
ago when I studied the story of Mary and Martha entertaining
Jesus in Luke 10.

I was Martha. I opened my home and wore myself out.
I, too, questioned why others didn't help. As I prayed and
pondered, I asked God to help me change into a Mary. And
gradually, I did.

I learned to plan ahead. My cupboard has ingredients
for casseroles and salads. I buy ice cream and cookies on sale
and always have crackers and cheese. An extra box of herbal
tea and a pound of coffee are on the shelf.

I learned to keep it simple. I've replaced five-course
dinners with casseroles. Usually, I serve fruit or ice cream
instead of pie. Often I invite folks for dessert. Restaurants
are great since there's no cleanup. Whether it's for a meal or
coffee, time together is what matters most.

I accept help. If my guests offer to bring dessert, I let them. Carrying is difficult for me because of physical problems, so now I ask guests to take the casserole from the oven to the table. Recently a missionary said, "I feel at home in your home. You treat me like family, not company."

LIVING OUT GOD'S PLAN FOR MY LIFE
Most importantly, I pray. As I set the table, I pray for each guest. While I prepare the food or drive to a restaurant, I ask God to guide our conversation. I've learned that hospitality is much more than bread.

BETTY LUNDBERG, www.bettylundberg.com

WHAT I LEARNED FROM GOD TODAY...

Yes, He Cares

The LORD shall preserve your going out and your coming in.
PSALM 121:8

I love this phrase: "The Lord shall preserve your going out
and your coming in" (Psalm 121:8).

Sometimes when I rise in the morning and take a good
look at the schedule blaring at me from my daily planner,
I sigh deeply and feel like a slave to the world's demands.
Do you ever feel that way? Go out, come in; go out, come in.
The days begin to look alike as they entangle themselves
into urgent appointments—this meeting, then the next one.
Yet God promises to preserve us even as we go out and come
in—which is, by the way, a wonderful Old Testament idiom
that expresses the regular routines of life.

This promise extends even deeper into the world of
everyday responsibilities. Maybe you have small children at
home. You look at the day and think, *Boy, this is just like yesterday. And yesterday was like the day before. All I do is get up
in the morning, take care of kids, wash clothes, clean up their
messes, prepare them for school, run errands all over town, come
home, make dinner, and fall in bed too tired even to sleep. Then
I get up the next morning and start all over again.* In your darker
moments you begin to wonder, *Is God involved in all of this?*

LIVING OUT GOD'S PLAN FOR MY LIFE

Does He care at all about the endless treadmill of my life? Let me assure you that He does care. He watches over you and preserves you in your going out and in your coming in. This is a promise that His Word repeats over and over, so that there may be no question about it. He cares.

DAVID JEREMIAH, *When Your World Falls Apart*

WHAT I LEARNED FROM GOD TODAY...

Self-Conscious to God-Conscious

I will praise You, for I am fearfully and
wonderfully made.... How precious also
are Your thoughts to me, O God!

PSALM 139:14, 17

I stood in line at the drinking fountain with my kindergarten classmates and was shocked to see beads of water covering my red sweater and dripping down the front of me. A boy had spit his mouthful on me and then gleefully ran away. I had done nothing to provoke him and was humiliated.

After living in a tension-filled home, an object of my dad's ridicule, I desperately needed to feel loved and accepted. I repeatedly re-lived the scene of the incident, compounding the rejection I felt.

At home, I walked on eggshells, hoping not to do anything to anger Dad. I became a shy, self-conscious perfectionist—always desiring to please and do the right thing to win Dad's approval. But, if I chose black, he wanted white. I was happy if he was happy with me, which was rare, and I was hurt and saddened when he wasn't.

In my mid-teens, I came to realize that my dad had a problem—some people can be critical no matter what. I learned that everyone isn't going to approve of me or my best efforts to do good. And it's okay. I needed to focus on what God thought of me.

Once I understood that God designed me as a unique individual, flaws and all, to be used for His purposes, my perspective changed. I'm special in God's eyes. He's my loving Father and wants the best for me (Psalm 139:13–17).

LIVING OUT GOD'S PLAN FOR MY LIFE

When "spit upon," I recognize such behavior as ungodly, stemming from a critical spirit. It's a tool of Satan to discourage me; to hinder me from being the confident, secure person God desires me to be.

If criticism is valid, I accept it and respond appropriately. But if it's malevolent, I dismiss it as a tactic of the enemy and quickly forgive the critic, who is either in rebellion or ignorant of being used as a vessel to promote discord. I remain peaceful, choosing to love those who stir up strife (1 Peter 2:21–23) (Romans 12:14; 17–21).

JILL DARLING, www.EditorialCoffee.com

WHAT I LEARNED FROM GOD TODAY...

_____

_____

_____

_____

_____

It's Not How Much We Own...

Then he said to the crowd, "Don't be greedy!
Owning a lot of things won't make your life safe."
LUKE 12:15

My wife Chris has said many times that it's sinful how many fishing lures, worms, and spinnerbaits we have. It scares me to think that Jesus just might agree with her. Perhaps even worse, we still keep getting more.

Jesus was never hung up on stuff. He sent His disciples out to preach with almost nothing but His Word. He wants us to have a relationship with Him and with the Father. He knows what this life is all about.

Two or three times during our forty years of marriage, Chris and I have come very close to losing everything, and I mean everything. We had accumulated so much stuff, but it was all about to go away. Once we were at peace with losing it all, God stepped in and saved us.

LIVING OUT GOD'S PLAN FOR MY LIFE

Life is measured by how much God owns us.

WHAT I LEARNED FROM GOD TODAY...

Life Is an Ocean

God is our refuge and strength,
an ever-present help in trouble.
Therefore we will not fear...though waters roar and foam....

PSALM 46:1–2,3 NIV

As a child, the ocean was not my friend. I may have been quick to spend a day in its midst, but there was never a feeling of trust between us. More than once, I found a wave upon me—monstrous, the crest breaking over my head; knocking me off my feet easily as if I were of no account, and hurtling me crazily, mercilessly into the sand. Then, never satisfied, it seemed to grow arms that reached and strangled, pulling me back into the black deepness, always ushering me against my will. Gasping, arms flailing, feet searching for firm ground, panic mounting as I struggled to get out of the clutches of the sadistic water. Almost succeeding, I would turn to find another wave rapidly descending: each wave bigger, always growing bigger.

I feel that same panic today as I view the problems of my life. One wave of problems follows another—each one more swollen and angry. There is too much on my schedule. Or it is time to let the children go. Or I must helplessly watch a loved one suffering by feeling overwhelmed, suffocating, wondering if I will ever get my head above water again.

It is time to stop bracing myself for the next impact. Instead, I will anchor my heart on the promise of the One in charge of my life.

Living out God's Plan for My Life
No matter how much noise the waters make around us, God has a voice of peace to calm our heart if we will take time to hear his Word and let his presence embrace us.

NANI BELL, www.EditorialCoffee.com

What I Learned from God Today...

Test All Things

Test all things; hold fast what is good.

I THESSALONIANS 5:21

The surprise came when I called Mack to follow up on the demo I'd given him. As Safety Director, Mack had already indicated his team liked our dock safety barrier design and had decided to purchase them. The barrier uses a steel I-beam to keep forklifts from accidentally driving out of elevated dock doors when there is no truck parked in them waiting to be loaded. Mack had allowed me to install a demonstration unit at one of their loading docks to use and evaluate.

Just to be sure all was still going well, I asked: "So Mack, the feedback from the dock attendants has been good and there aren't any concerns or comments?"

There was a slight pause. "Oh yeah, real positive, I am very satisfied that it works!" After another pause, he added, "We drove a forklift into it!"

"What?" I nearly shouted, feeling shocked. "What do you mean you drove into it? Was there an accident? What happened?" I knew the barrier would work; it had been tested and had saved lives in the past, but if an accident had occurred I would have expected a phone call right away.

Mack explained, "We parked a trailer in an open dock door. I got on the forklift and rammed it into the barrier. It was fine. We had to know that it would work—it's my job to know."

LIVING OUT GOD'S PLAN FOR MY LIFE

Mack needed to know for himself that all my sales assertions were totally reliable for the safety of others. He took personal responsibility to "test all things" for those who trusted in his judgment and recommendation.

As believers, we need to show the same diligence in the things we preach, teach, and recommend that others follow in the interest of their spiritual safety.

JOHN MATUSZAK, www.dockbarrier.com

WHAT I LEARNED FROM GOD TODAY...

You Can Start Over

Commit to the LORD whatever you do,
And your plans will succeed.

PROVERBS 16:3, NIV

P eople frequently ask me how I met my husband,
Robert Schuller. I don't mind repeating the story, because
it is the perfect example of God's hand in helping us to start
over when we've hit a dead end. Now matter how hopeless
or dark our lives become, God has a plan to bring us back
into the light. This is what happened to both Robert and me
when our paths crossed.

At that time in my life, starting over wasn't an option—
it was a necessity. My husband of only a few years decided
he no longer wanted to be married! It was a low point for
me, a time when I felt as if all my hopes and dreams had
been stripped from me.

I first saw Robert Schuller in the parking garage of our
apartment building. He was carrying a very large briefcase,
and I assumed he was a door-to-door salesman. I would
learn later that he was indeed a kind of salesman! He was a
minister, so he sold hope, faith, and God's love—things I
certainly needed at this low point in my life.

But he was starting over too, and that greatly appealed
to me. Right from the beginning, there was a mutual respect

and admiration for each other. Somehow I just knew that
God had brought us together.

LIVING OUT GOD'S PLAN FOR MY LIFE

Love had delivered me a new life. It was a huge life with
enormous responsibilities, and—prepared or not—I had
signed up for it! But God never gives us more than we can
handle, and he has been faithful to Robert and me. Just
recently we celebrated twenty-two years of marriage.

God takes the brokenness in our lives, and through His
love He forgives and He heals. He builds us—if we let Him
into our hearts. Have the faith and humility to let Him in!

DONNA SCHULLER, *Woman to Woman Wisdom*

WHAT I LEARNED FROM GOD TODAY . . .

Getting Outside Myself

Serve the LORD with gladness;
Come before His presence with singing.
Know that the LORD, He is God;
It is He who has made us, and not we ourselves....

PSALM 100:2–3

Pulling out of me has been some of the healthiest and most liberating steps I've taken. My life had become too much about me. How was I feeling? What made me comfortable? Did I feel safe? My constant introspection kept me in knots and caused me to be self-serving. While it's good to take care of one's self, too much of anything becomes nauseating.

So I began to find ways to serve my family. At first I did spontaneous favors like serving my husband, Les, coffee, bringing in the newspaper for him, or making bread pudding, which is his favorite dessert. Sometimes I would run him a bath and lay out his clothes as a thoughtful surprise or offer him a head massage or a backrub.

I concentrated on spending time with our son, Marty, doing things he loved. One of his passions was putting together hundred-piece puzzles. So he and I would have contests to see who could assemble his or her puzzle first. Then we would celebrate the winner with bowls of buttered popcorn.

At Christmas Les, Marty, and I would pack boxes in

62

our home for Salvation Army families and deliver them on Christmas Eve. It was our way of stepping out of our meager situation to think of others, who were having even tougher times.

LIVING OUT GOD'S PLAN FOR MY LIFE
I found the simplest of acts could help me get my mind off of myself while improving my relationships with others.

PATSY CLAIRMONT, *I Grew Up Little*

WHAT I LEARNED FROM GOD TODAY...

After the Funeral

Therefore encourage one another and build each other up....

1 THESSALONIANS 5:11, NIV

I used to make quick funeral home visits, sign the book, and send a sympathy card.

If I knew the grieving well and it was convenient, I'd take food in a disposable dish. (I didn't want the sorrowing returning my dish and crying in my kitchen).

That changed when my mother died. I learned how much kindness is appreciated after the funeral. Close friends took me to lunch and I talked all afternoon. Another friend gave me flowers. Hand-written notes were appreciated. I felt less alone as others reached out.

Now I stay longer at the funeral home. I hug the grieving and tell them I'm praying. I give food in a disposable dish because it's easier for them, not me.

About a week after the funeral I write to the grieving and share memories. My note includes, "I'm praying for you."

A couple of weeks after the funeral I take the grieving to lunch. We usually go early afternoon and sit in a quiet corner. I ask, "How are you doing?" Listening is important, and I've heard good and bad memories. I reassure the hurting of my prayer support.

Throughout the first year I send notes on special days.

Birthdays, Christmas, and Valentine's Day are lonely. Mother's Day is still difficult for me. I write to friends who have lost their mother that year. (I do the same for Father's Day.) On the anniversary of the death I send a note.

I've learned caring needs to continue after the funeral.

LIVING OUT GOD'S PLAN FOR MY LIFE

Whether I have received comfort or given comfort, I have been blessed.

BETTY LUNDBERG, www.bettylundberg.com

WHAT I LEARNED FROM GOD TODAY...

God's Masterpiece

I pray also that the eyes of your heart
may be enlightened in order that you may know
the hope to which he has called you, the riches
of his glorious inheritance in the saints....

EPHESIANS 1:18, NIV

One of my favorite places is at Sedona, a colorful masterpiece of 350 million years of creation. It is truly a place of intoxicating splendor, from the spectacular majestic red rock sculptures to the panoramic sunsets and garnet-colored skies, where clouds float like tufts of cotton balls. Whenever my physical eyes need to feed my spiritual eyes, I head there. From the moment I arrive, I can just feel the peace edging out the stress and strain of too much time in my office, and in the airport—and, well, with too many people!

I was just in Sedona this past weekend. I checked into my log-cabin-style accommodations and immediately headed to the water's edge, the lovely tumbling waters of Oak Creek. I have a tendency to mostly travel at the speed of light, but not in Sedona. Sitting there feeding the ducks, I note the precise moment when the fuchsia sun drops below the horizon; when a sliver of moon winks itself into violet sky; and then, when a full heaven of stars comes sliding into view. You really can sit still that long in Sedona, in a stillness that has a voice of its own. Always I assign this incredible sense of serenity to God. Do you have a place like this, a place that infuses you with the incomparable supremacy of the great Creator?

LIVING OUT GOD'S PLAN FOR MY LIFE

Yes, the wonder and beauty of nature leaves us with a feeling of awe and tranquility, but it does more: in nature we are reunited with larger truths—we live in a world of creation. But being filled with an appreciation for the wonder and beauty of nature is not about telling ourselves what a great and wondrous world we live in, but rather that this, too, is just a part of the fullness of God.

BETTIE B. YOUNGS, *Woman to Woman Wisdom*

WHAT I LEARNED FROM GOD TODAY...

Mirror the Light

But if we walk in the light as He is in the light,
we have fellowship with one another,
and the blood of Jesus Christ His Son cleanses us from all sin.

D o you remember what you learned in high school science class about the four ways substances react to light? Some are *transparent*, which means light passes through them. Others are *translucent*, which means they scatter light. Still other substances are *opaque*, which means they block light. And then there are *mirrors*, which reflect light. I'm sure you've noticed...

There are lots of transparent people, who seem oblivious to the Light.

There are countless translucent people, who make the Light very confusing.

There are even more opaque people, who are dead-set against the Light.

But, praise God, there are a few mirrorlike people who reflect the Light.

LIVING OUT GOD'S PLAN FOR MY LIFE

God has called us all to be mirrors, to reflect His Light to the world. The fact that you've been on a hard road and survived by walking with Him means you have a lot of Light to reflect.

MARK ATTEBERRY, *Walking with God on the Road You Never Wanted to Travel*

WHAT I LEARNED FROM GOD TODAY . . .

Under New Management

Therefore, if anyone is in Christ, he is a new creation;
old things have passed away;
behold, all things have become new.

2 CORINTHIANS 5:17

When we turn our heart over to Jesus as our Savior, it's like a restaurant hanging out a sign that says "Under New Management." Things have changed inside. Our heart becomes new, just as God's Word tells us, but the surrounding neighborhood doesn't always change right away. As we seek to follow Him, we'll find new ways to interact within our old setting. When we start "making over" our own establishment and attracting a different group of friends, our surroundings may gradually change as well. We may find that people who weren't welcome in our lives are now the ones we seek out for fellowship, and some negative hangers-on from our past life lose interest as they watch our world transformed into something with which they are unfamiliar. Some people will come to understand the changes and be transformed along with us.

Ultimately, we take on the responsibility to direct our lives, and this influences everything around us, just as a new restaurant can set a run-down neighborhood on the road to rehab and a positive community.

LIVING OUT GOD'S PLAN FOR MY LIFE

We can become part of God's extreme makeover team to the circumstances and people around us when we let his Word and Holy Spirit transform our own lives first. People might not like our "new menu" at first, but those who are hungry for God will "taste and see" that He is good (Psalm 34:8).

PAT MATUSZAK, www.EditorialCoffee.com

WHAT I LEARNED FROM GOD TODAY...

The Grumble Bug

Talk of all His wondrous works! Glory in His holy name....
Remember His marvelous works which He has done....

I Chronicles 16:9–10, 12

The grumble bug used to bite me more frequently than I care to admit. When my business was booming, I fussed about not having enough time to myself. When it slacked off, I bemoaned the bills stacking to the ceiling. If a customer arrived late, I groaned because they upset my schedule. If someone arrived early, I griped because she interrupted my free time.

The rash of discontentment spread to other areas—disturbances with my family and friends, annoyance with the church, and turbulence with the weather. Regardless of the situation, the itch to complain irritated me and I opened the wound with my digging remarks.

Recently, I discovered a "bug" repellent in I Chronicles 16:9–12. When I was running my mouth with complaints, I failed to remember His marvelous works, His wonders, and the judgments of His mouth. Since I began to fill the air with thanksgiving and praises to the Lord, the grumble bug keeps his distance. While I talk about God's wondrous works, the grumble bug can't bite. In fact, it can't even light.

Living out God's Plan for My Life

Occasionally, I neglect to use the formula and the grumble bug takes advantage of my exposed flesh. But as soon as I call on the name of the Lord, He applies the balm that soothes the itch to bellyache about my circumstances.

Learning to spend my time concentrating on the Lord has freed me from the grumble bug's torment.

BRENDA K. HENDRICKS, www.EditorialCoffee.com

What I Learned from God Today...

Overcoming Labels

[Jesus said] "These things I have spoken to you,
that in Me you may have peace.
In the world you will have tribulation;
but be of good cheer, I have overcome the world."

JOHN 16:33

Labeling has caused people to feel shamed, defeated, or inadequate because they've been judged and now have been programmed to think of themselves as bad, unacceptable, unfair, abnormal, incapable, irredeemable, or less worthy of blessing than other people on the planet. This low self-esteem, this poor self-image, this mind-set that marks you as "unworthy" is a lie. It's faulty programming. God is not a past-performance God; He's an unconditionally loving, past-forgotten, "Let's step boldly together into the future" God. If you take just one minute and change the label you and others have placed on you, you can begin to change your life in that same minute.

A parent who loses a child faces one of the worst tragedies imaginable. Few people would be surprised if that parent ended up clinically depressed or addicted to drugs—prescription or otherwise. By contrast, though, many people who have faced that kind of heartbreaking loss have used their experiences as a catalyst to establish some of the greatest charities, foundations, and support groups in the world today. Those people turned their stress-inducing tragedies into life-changing missions.

Living out God's Plan for My Life

To live in congruency with your God-given nature is to be an overcomer—an overcomer with a purpose and mission.

Dr. Ben Lerner with Dr. Greg Loman,
One-Minute Wellness

What I Learned from God Today...

Why Should I Fear
When the Evil Day Comes?

Why should I fear in the days of evil?

PSALM 49:5

Taking care of my father, who is suffering in the last stages of Alzheimer's along with a seizure disorder, is cause for dread and worry. What could the Psalmist be thinking in the 49th Psalm, implying I should not to be afraid?

My dad earned a master's degree from Duke University, chose to give up the pastorate of a large church, and gave his life as a missionary. Today he is completely bedridden, the dreaded Alzheimer's having robbed him of his memories and his independence, always on the verge of another seizure.

What did the Psalmist know that I have missed?

It would help if God were predictable. Dad has served God faithfully, so it seems right that God would give Dad a fruitful life to the end. But God does what He wants and answers to no one. How do I fearlessly trust a God who does not play by *my* idea of rules of fairness and happiness?

I cannot explain why the Psalmist is right, but I know it for a fact. Each morning as I awaken Dad for medicines and bathing, it is evident: God's mercies are "new every morning" (Lamentations 3:23). As unbelievable as it sounds, these are not dark days at Dad's bedside. Dad may have forgotten God, but God has not forgotten my dad.

Living out God's Plan for My Life
Why should I fear when the evil day comes? There is no reason to fear: God is here even in the evil day, and He is enough!

NANI BELL, www.EditorialCoffee.com

What I Learned from God Today...

Moments of Grace

*Walk in love, as Christ also has loved us
and given Himself for us....*

EPHESIANS 5:2

I'm at an airport restaurant. A marine sits across from me,
alone, almost finished with his meal. A couple, about the
age his parents might be, stops and visits with him for a while.
Where is he stationed? they ask. Where is he headed? How
long has it been since he's been home? Before leaving, the
gentleman tells the marine he would consider it an honor if
he could pick up his dinner tab. He shakes the marine's hand
and thanks him for serving our country. And just when I
think the woman is going to lean down and give the marine
a hug, he stands up instead.

The next moment is like a Norman Rockwell painting.
The marine is tall, the woman petite. He stoops to give her a
hug. Arms around each other, she is patting his shoulder as
any mother would do to comfort her son.

Just everyday happenings, but the moments are magical.

It's hard to realize that little gestures can make much of
a difference in people's lives. But I imagine that if we were to
ask the couple or the marine, they would tell us such things
really do matter.

LIVING OUT GOD'S PLAN FOR MY LIFE

There's something about an unexpected kindness in our not-too-kind world that brightens a day and pokes a hole in the darkness.

ALICE GRAY, *Small Acts of Grace*

WHAT I LEARNED FROM GOD TODAY...

Work Six Days, Rest One Day

He makes me to lie down in green pastures;
He leads me beside the still waters. He restores my soul.

PSALM 23:2–3

Take time to replenish what has been depleted in your life. At times we need to rest. To rest physically means to sleep, to exert ourselves less, to attempt fewer physical chores. It might mean we need to go less and stay home more. To rest emotionally and mentally means to stop thinking about some things so much. It doesn't mean we stop caring, but it might mean we do stop caring so much. We turn our cares over to the Lord, asking the Lord to take care of the person in ways we cannot. To rest spiritually is to trust God to provide for us and others what we are wearing ourselves out trying to provide!

If you are depleted spiritually, then you need to take time to replenish yourself spiritually. If you are depleted emotionally, you need to do those things that fill you up emotionally. If you are depleted physically, you need to do what's necessary to restore your body.

God designed us to have a day of praise and thanks and quiet mediation on His Word. He designed us to have a day in which we gather with others to praise and give thanks and to study His Word. God "rested" on the seventh day of creation, not because He was tired but because He was setting into motion by example His desire that man experience restoration, replenishment, and refreshment.

LIVING OUT GOD'S PLAN FOR MY LIFE

God designed us to have a rhythm in our lives in which we have a time totally devoted to restoring what has been given out, replenishing what has been used up, receiving back what has been spent, and refreshing what has grown stale. He designed us so that our deepest form of restoration, replenishment, and refreshment is to come in relationship to Him.

PAULA WHITE, *A Sensational Life*

WHAT I LEARNED FROM GOD TODAY...

Humility

If my people, which are called by my name,
shall humble themselves, and pray,
and seek my face, and turn from their wicked ways;
then will I hear from heaven, and will forgive their sin.

2 CHRONICLES 7:14, KJV

Humility is an attitude. It is an inner system of caution we should use to evaluate ourselves before the Lord. The Lord is high and lifted up, and we are supposed to take a position of lowliness. We think of the apostle Paul as assertive, bold, and confrontational. He was not passive. When Peter was compromising, Paul "opposed him to his face" (Galatians 2:11). This evangelist, strategist, and architect of church history seems anything but humble. Yet that was the quality he claimed for himself and preached to us (Philippians 4:7–8).

Paul reminded the Corinthians of his painful service: "All right, you Corinthians, I want to tell you my personal experience. I was whipped five times. I was beaten with rods three times. I was let down by a wall in a basket. I was stoned. I've been imprisoned. I've been naked. I've been lonely. I've been shipwrecked three times. I've been hungry. I've been deprived. I've been betrayed by other people" (2 Corinthians 11:23–33). Yet, at the end of his ministry this man could say, "I'm the least of all the saints" (see Ephesians 3:8).

The apostle James warned his readers against favoritism, a subtle form of pride. "If you show special attention to the man wearing fine clothes and say, 'Here's a good seat for you,' but say to the poor man, 'You stand there' or 'Sit on the floor by my feet,' have you not discriminated among yourselves and become judges with evil thoughts?" (James 2:1–4). I'll tell you what: those who are lowly God will exalt, and those who are rich God will put down. They will be like the flower of the field, and they will wither and die and blow away—they'll perish (James 1:9–11).

LIVING OUT GOD'S PLAN FOR MY LIFE

This is one of God's absolutely reliable principles for life: "If my people, which are called by my name, shall humble themselves, and pray, and seek my face, and turn from their wicked ways; then I will hear from heaven, and will forgive their sin" (2 Chronicles 7:14). That's the power of humility, the power of taking the proper position before the Lord, and serving the Lord with humility of mind.

FRANKLIN GRAHAM WITH ROSS RHOADS, *All for Jesus*

WHAT I LEARNED FROM GOD TODAY...

A Father's Lessons about God

In Him was life, and the life was the light of men.

JOHN 1:4

My dad taught me a lot about life and seemed to have wisdom for just about any situation. He gave advice on the practical side of life: how to write out my first check, to find the carton of eggs without any broken ones, to ride a bike, drive a car, and interview for a job. The presence of God in his heart was most precious; it gave him peace in any circumstance, a kind word and a sense of humor that always caused others to smile. My dad had an unshakable faith that his hand was always holding God's.

One of the sweetest ways my dad reminded me of the heavenly Father part of God happened after saying our "goodnights." My dad would always return to the living room with a flashlight, set it down beside me, and say, "In case the power goes out." Over time, he didn't have to say anything. He quietly set the flashlight down beside me and I'd turn from the TV, smile, and say, "Thanks, Dad." He never stopped being a father. Even after I was grown, he still wanted to make sure his kid wouldn't stumble in the dark, lose her way, or be afraid of what she couldn't see in the night. He made sure I had light for the way.

God has done the same. He gave us His only Son as the

light of the world. We often become distracted in life with our own ideas, agendas, and routines, but God is faithful and has provided us with the hand of His Son.

LIVING OUT GOD'S PLAN FOR MY LIFE

Just like my dad, God doesn't want us to stumble in the dark, lose our way, or be afraid when we can't see the way ahead either. Though the power may not go out, our dreams sometimes die, our hopes may fade, and our journey can seem dark and difficult. He has made a way for us to reach for the light…not just a flashlight…the true Light of the World.

My dad no longer walks this earthly path. He's home now in the glorious light of the Father's presence. I am so thankful for the gift I had in my dad. It makes me smile to imagine that if God ever needed to explain what a godly father should be like on earth, He could have pointed to my dad and said, "That's what I mean."

DORI MAGEE, www.EditorialCoffee.com

What I Learned from God Today...

Jesus as Friend

For when I am weak, then I am strong.

2 CORINTHIANS 12:10

I began to discover the real me, not through my talents and successes, but when I started embracing my weaknesses and realized I don't have to hold it all together. I *can't* hold it all together. I don't have to have it all figured out. If I did, I would have no need for God. And I sensed that somewhere, wrapped up in the deep recesses of my pain, there was a purpose. I was ready to discover it.

No more hiding. No more running. No more clenching. I had finally let go.

My concept of Jesus was so big that it lacked the personal; instead of focusing on a close connection with Him, I had worked long and hard on those relationships I could manipulate through my "Look at me, aren't I great!" mentality. That is why bulimia seemed like such a good option for me for so long—because I believed bulimia kept me thin, and I thought people accepted me more readily when I looked a certain way.

I cannot explain how freeing it was when I embraced Christ as my real Friend. For so long He was simply a gigantic *idea* to me. Although I believed them to be true, the unfathomable images of Savior, Redeemer, and the ultimate sacrifice for mankind made God so big in my mind that what I knew of Him didn't translate to what was going on in my everyday life.

LIVING OUT GOD'S PLAN FOR MY LIFE

I had always been told of God's great love, and somewhere inside I believed it. But what completely melted my heart, what completely liberated me from choking insecurity, wasn't just the truth that Jesus loved me but that Jesus liked me. He LIKED me! Exactly as I was. I didn't have to pretend; I didn't have to be a certain size or wear the right jeans. I could be having a bad-hair day, and He would still like me.

NATALIE GRANT, *The Real Me*

WHAT I LEARNED FROM GOD TODAY...

God's Gentle Embrace

Grace and peace be multiplied to you
in the knowledge of God and of Jesus our Lord.

2 PETER 1:2

You can label me a zoo-aholic. I love to visit the zoo and observe God's amazing creation. My girls, on the other hand, were zooed-out by the time they were seven years old, because I insisted on dragging them to every zoo in every city we ever visited. Now that my kids have grown out of zoo-age, I'm waiting for the grandkids. We still have a few years to go!

What do you like most when you visit the zoo? Personally, I take great joy in observing the newborns; the baby chimp playing with its mother, the sweet little lamb standing next to the woolly ewe, the squealing piglets snuggling up against the big mother sow. Not too long ago a baby elephant was born at our local zoo. Watching the super-sized baby lovingly interacting with its mother was an amazing sight!

Have you ever pictured yourself nestled in the divine embrace of your Heavenly Father? The Bible says, "He tends his flock like a shepherd; He gathers the lambs in his arms and carries them close to his heart; he gently leads those that have young." Isn't that a wonderful picture of the tender love and care God wants to demonstrate toward us and our families?

Living out God's Plan for My Life

As a mom, I often feel frazzled, worried, and worn; yet when I take my cares to my Heavenly Father in prayer, I sense His loving arms wrapping gently around me, and I hear the beat of His heart.

KAROL LADD, *A Positive Plan for Creating More Calm, Less Stress*

What I Learned from God Today . . .

Reach Out

*You yourselves are our letter, written on our hearts,
known and read by everyone. You show that
you are a letter from Christ . . . not written with ink but
with the Spirit of the living God,
not on tablets of stone but on tablets of human hearts.*

2 CORINTHIANS 3:2–4, NIV

Hold up your testimony for other people's sake. I have
lost count of how many times people have told me,
"I was ready to give up because my trials were so hard, but
when I heard your story, I said, 'If Tammy can go through
all that, I can make it through my troubles.'" We have all
suffered in this world to some degree. Those of us who have
experienced deep loss need the comfort of others who have
gone before us. Somehow that makes the fight a little easier.
We all have a place where our testimony is a light in the
darkness to those who need to hear a word of encouragement
or see a person who is standing strong in the face of difficulty.
Even if they are not in need of your advice today, people will
remember your story when they face trials in the future.

Living out God's Plan for My Life

Remember that young people are watching. You are a mentor and one who holds up a standard against the darkness of this world in which they live. How can your testimony change the world around you for God? Your home? Your school? Your workplace? It only takes a small candle to light up a whole room that is in darkness. You don't have to have a great singing voice or eloquent speech to say a few encouraging words that will open up someone's heart to healing. Sometimes no words are necessary—a smile or a friendly hand on someone's shoulder is all that is needed to turn their day around or, better yet, their life!

TAMMY TRENT, *Beyond the Sorrow*

What I Learned from God Today...

Touch of Forgiveness

And be kind to one another, tenderhearted,
forgiving one another, even as God in Christ forgave you..

EPHESIANS 4:32

A loving touch is so healing. It is often more comforting than words. I still remember the gentle touch of my mother's hand on my forehead whenever I was sick. Just her touch made me feel better. It always reassured me of her love and took away any fears I had. Unfortunately, many people experience just the opposite. They associate touch with brutality or shame, often leaving them terrified of touch.

I remember when I was awakened many nights by my mother's screams, as my father violently attacked her in her sleep. I watched helplessly, an eight-year-old child crying at the top of the stairs, as I heard my mother begging for mercy. Though she suffered severe injuries and mental stress, God gave her the strength to make some hard decisions.

Did I grow up to hate my father? She wouldn't let me. She taught me the power of God's love in forgiveness. Years later as my father faced death, it was her hand he reached for, a hand that offered forgiveness.

Many live in abusive relationships until they find the courage to make right choices. The Lord has taught me through a courageous mother that forgiveness brings healing.

People tell me that there's a healing touch in my hands. I love that, because I know that a heart of forgiveness produces a healing touch.

Thanks, Mom!

LIVING OUT GOD'S PLAN FOR MY LIFE

Is there a painful memory that lets you know there's someone you need to forgive? Do it now, and allow the healing touch of Jesus to bring you comfort and peace.

JUDY BUFFUM-HEMMILA, www.crossfire-ministries.org

WHAT I LEARNED FROM GOD TODAY...

Inside the Walls

*And in that day it shall be
that living waters shall flow from Jerusalem....*

ZECHARIAH 14:7–9

In ancient times, the sentries of a city would bring news of approaching invaders. The city walls would quickly be fortified, and everyone would seek safety inside. What do you think the greatest fear would be in such a situation? It wasn't catapults or rocks or flaming spears. The people most feared being cut off from supplies of food or water. The invaders may not be able to come inside, but they could stop you from getting the things you needed from the outside.

"There is a river whose streams shall make glad the city of God, the holy place of the tabernacle of the Most High" (Psalm 46:4).

The meaning and symbolism of water in the Bible run deep—no pun intended. God's Spirit is ever present in our midst to refresh us, cleanse us, and strengthen us for the journey. He is the eternal spring that never runs dry. Jesus sat by a well one day and said, "Whoever drinks of this water will thirst again, but whoever drinks of the water that I shall give him will never thirst. But the water that I shall give him will become in him a fountain of water springing up unto everlasting life" (John 4:13–14).

Soon after that, Jesus said, "If anyone thirsts, let him come to Me and drink. He who believes in Me, as the Scripture has said, out of his heart will flow rivers of living water" (John 7:37–38).

LIVING OUT GOD'S PLAN FOR MY LIFE

The Holy Spirit of God living within you is a secret fountain of life-giving water. People don't realize the depth of God's Spirit in residence within your soul. Through the Holy Spirit, God has come to live inside you. There's no way to overstate the powerful implications of that startling truth. Almighty God is among us and within us. He is the source of living water, springing up into eternal life.

DAVID JEREMIAH, *When Your World Falls Apart*

WHAT I LEARNED FROM GOD TODAY...

Our Deepest Need

But God demonstrates His own love for us,
in that while we were still sinners, Christ died for us.

ROMANS 5:8

Forgiveness is every person's deepest need and the greatest quality of being like Jesus. The premise of forgiveness is sinfulness. Where there is no transgression there is no need for forgiveness. When there is the denial of God and absolutes of right and wrong, there is no desire for forgiveness because it is presumed that there is no offense. This is the death of conscience.

The obstacle to forgiveness is that the person is unwilling to admit his offense. This is the scourge of the human race. This is why God's love and the giving of His Son to die for the sins of the world is so amazing. Christ died for the ungodly (Romans 5:8). Forgiveness is all about Jesus and Jesus alone. God forgives only because Jesus took my sin and its judgment on the cross. He took in His body our sins so that we could live unto righteousness (1 Peter 2:24) and made us holy and without blame before Him in His love (Ephesians 1:4).

Jesus' forgiveness of us is the reason why we forgive others. Every time we forgive others, deserving it or not, we have a reminder of God's forgiveness. The last words Jesus gave to

His disciples were to preach "repentance and forgiveness of sins," sending them knowing that they had forgiveness by his blood, and cleansing from all sin (Luke 24:47; 1 John 1:7).

LIVING OUT GOD'S PLAN FOR MY LIFE

Of all the virtues of Jesus, of all the power in His name, there is nothing that exceeds His eternal absolution of all sin and from all judgment, His forgiveness of a person who believes and receives Him as Savior and Lord.

FRANKLIN GRAHAM WITH ROSS RHOADS, *All for Jesus*

WHAT I LEARNED FROM GOD TODAY...

God Knows the Way I Take

But He knows the way that I take;
When He has tested me, I shall come forth as gold.

JOB 23:10

In my Bible, I've circled and underlined the first part of
Job 23:10 and drawn a heart around the word *knows*.
That word is especially important to me because sometimes
I find myself wondering if the One who knows when every
sparrow falls to the ground really knows what I am going
through. I feel like the little toddler in children's church last
Sunday who reached up and turned my cheek in his direc-
tion and said, "Teacher, look at me."

Haven't we all wished God was near enough that we
could touch His cheek, turn it in our direction, and say,
"God, look at me." Perhaps Job felt that way too.

And yet despite his doubts, Job must still have trusted
God's heart. For right in the middle of his forsaken lament,
Job makes this incredible statement: "But He knows the way
that I take."

At his darkest moment, when the storm was raging and the
waves were crashing, Job had an anchor: *God knows about me.*

LIVING OUT GOD'S PLAN FOR MY LIFE

If you are tossed on the waves of hurt and the circumstances seem pitch-black, you have that anchor too. If you long to touch God's cheek and say, "Look at me," you can trust that His face is already turned toward you. His love is before you, behind you, and over you. You are enclosed by God!

ALICE GRAY, *Treasures for Women Who Hope*

WHAT I LEARNED FROM GOD TODAY...

A Passion to Know God

"The one who comes to Me I will by no means cast out."

JOHN 6:37

A fine Christian young man bluntly said to me, "Well, this is as good as I'm gonna be and as far as I'm gonna go." That was the first time I had heard someone come right out and say, "Don't count on me for any more than this. This is as good as I'm gonna be."

Whenever you draw a line between you and the Lord Jesus over any issue, you have chosen failure. By refusing to put something on the altar for Christ, however small it may be, we limit our relationship with Him and shut out the very source of our lives. If there is anything in your life that means more to you than Christ, you will never know the fullness of His love. Because God loves you, He will discipline you. Ultimately you might yield to Him, or perhaps you will insist on having your way and die without attaining your highest reward in life.

LIVING OUT GOD'S PLAN FOR MY LIFE

Nothing pleases God more than our full surrender, and He rewards it abundantly. God says, "The one who comes to Me I will certainly not cast out" (John 6:37, NASB). It is never God's fault when our relationship with Him wanes. More than anything else our Father in heaven wants an }intimate relationship with His children.

DR. CHARLES STANLEY, *Living the Extraordinary Life*

WHAT I LEARNED FROM GOD TODAY...

What We Have in Common

"My prayer is not for them alone. I pray also for those who will believe in me through their message, that all of them may be one, Father, just as you are in me and I am in you."

JOHN 17:20–21, NIV

We are different people...with different personalities... with different perspectives...from different places... having different plans and different pasts...scarred by different pains. Add to that different cultures and generations and it's no wonder we don't understand each other most of the time.

Then God places us together and says, "Let them be one." Let them be one?!!!

God gives us different gifts, so "being one" cannot mean having the same strengths.

God gives us different personalities and preferences, so "being one" cannot mean having identical ideas.

The infinitely creative God has made us infinitely different, so "being one" cannot mean the absence of diversity.

So what does it mean? I'd like to suggest that "being one" is not about the absence of difference but about the presence of commitment. We are committed to one another as an overflow of our commitment to Jesus.

LIVING OUT GOD'S PLAN FOR MY LIFE

What knits us together as Christians is not that we are homogenous people, but that we are His people. Not that we all agree but that we all believe.

ALICIA BRITT CHOLE, *Pure Joy!*

WHAT I LEARNED FROM GOD TODAY...

Divine Connections

He heals the brokenhearted and binds up their wounds.

PSALM 147:3, NIV

Music brings a divine connection between heaven and earth. When I sing, I feel so close to the Lord. It has a way of lifting me into a place where I'm safe and beyond the reach of pain. I get lost in the Presence of God, where I find peace of mind, even in the most stressful times.

Years ago I was head of women's ministries for a large church. The night before one of our biggest conferences, I was called into the pastor's office. It was there that I learned of my husband's infidelity for the last fifteen years of our marriage. We had been leaders in the church for sixteen years. In shock and indescribable stomach and chest pain, I wrapped my arms around myself to keep from shattering into a million pieces.

People's words echoed faintly in the room, as they discussed canceling or continuing the conference. The voice of my own thoughts grew louder than theirs: "My God! My God! I can't breathe—this isn't real. Please, somebody wake me up!" I wondered how I could possibly lead the conference now.

I learned that His grace is all we need to face impossible situations. I opened the conference with a prayer and a song. As I sang, I could feel God's strength coming into me, and by His grace many women were ministered to, including me. The ladies didn't know what had happened until years later, but Jesus did. Through the ministry of music, he brought me into a place of healing.

LIVING OUT GOD'S PLAN FOR MY LIFE

If you are hurting and it feels like your world is crumbling beneath you, reach up to your heavenly Father and let music lift you into His healing arms.

JUDY BUFFUM-HEMMILA, www.crossfire-ministries.org

WHAT I LEARNED FROM GOD TODAY...

Pursue the Dream

We have this treasure in earthen vessels,
that the excellence of the power may be of God and not of us.

2 CORINTHIANS 4:7

There's no difference between your "true" self and God's plan for you. Your true self is made up of your deepest desires and gifts and abilities and dreams and passions. Your true self is what God created in you. It is who God made you to be.

Selfishness is not a matter of pursuing your true self. Selfishness is when you stop giving to others and when you keep all of the harvest you reap for your own pleasures.

Instead of accepting the limits that have been placed on you (including the limits you have placed on yourself), challenge the system and pursue your passion!

You are not a product of what has happened to you or what other people have said about you. You are the sum total of what is in you and Who is in you.

God's Word says, "We have this treasure in earthen vessels, that the excellence of the power may be of God and not of us" (2 Corinthians 4:7). What God has put in you is treasure. That word in the Greek means a deposit of wealth... of value.

Living Out God's Plan for My Life

Treasure is what God has given you as your gifts and talents. It is the Spirit that God has placed in you.

Why do you have this treasure? That the "excellence of the power of God" might be manifested in your life.

PAULA WHITE, *A Sensational Life*

What I Learned from God Today...

_____

_____

_____

_____

_____

_____

_____

_____

_____

_____

_____

_____

Heavenly Superstore

*Now to Him who is able to do exceedingly abundantly
above all that we ask or think, according to the power that
works in us, to Him be glory in the church by Christ Jesus
to all generations, forever and ever. Amen.*

EPHESIANS 3:20–21

God has surprises in store for us that we can't even imagine. I've tried to imagine heaven, but from what the Bible teaches it may be beyond my imagination. Maybe seeing heaven will be similar to what happened to a family we befriended after they arrived in the United States from Poland in the 1980s. They were amazed at the abundance here. Their first trip to an American supermarket was one surprise after another.

Their first surprise was that we did not have to wait in line to get into the store. They were used to waiting for hours in line for a loaf of bread. Inside, the couple could not believe the number of choices available and asked me if it would be all right to buy two of each item.

"Sure, you can buy five if you want," I laughed. I paid for our cartload with a check, but when the bag boy handed me a claim tag and pushed the cart off to meet us at the curbside loading area, their faces fell. Across our language barrier I tried to reassure my worried friends that we would see our groceries again, but it was clear that they thought we'd been refused and were headed home empty-handed. When I pulled the car around to the curb and the bag boy began to load our items into the trunk, the couple actually broke into a cheer. "Oh, I understand!" the husband laughed. "I cannot believe it!" They laughed all the way home.

Living out God's Plan for My Life

I think we will say something like that when we see the surprise of heaven's glory:

"Oh, I understand! I didn't believe it could be this good!"

What do you imagine heaven will be like? It will be even better in living color! In fact, our whole definition of "living color" may rise to a new level.

Pat Matuszak, www.EditorialCoffee.com

What I Learned from God Today...

_____

_____

_____

_____

_____

_____

Substitutes

Behold, to obey is better than sacrifice....

1 SAMUEL 15:22

I *nstead of buttermilk, use yogurt.*
   Instead of lemon juice, use vinegar...."

The cookbook's substitution chart provides a useful list of replacements for common ingredients.

When dealing with food, substitution is smart. But substitution is sabotage when dealing with the heart.

Instructed to destroy everything associated with the Amalekites' idolatrous culture, King Saul preserved the best of the spoils. He explained to Samuel that he disobeyed in order "to sacrifice to the LORD" (1 Samuel 15:21). But no sacrifice can substitute for obedience.

King Saul's substitution sabotaged his reign. Substitutions can likewise sabotage our futures. God asks for commitment, we offer excuses. God asks for purity, we substitute activity. God asks for time, we substitute money. God asks for love, we substitute things.

LIVING OUT GOD'S PLAN FOR MY LIFE

The recipe for bringing God delight reads simply:
1 heart of obedience *(no substitutions allowed).*

ALICIA BRITT CHOLE, *Pure Joy!*

WHAT I LEARNED FROM GOD TODAY...

_____

_____

_____

_____

_____

_____

_____

_____

_____

_____

_____

_____

_____

_____

Hopeful Future

"For I know the plans I have for you,"
declares the LORD, "plans to prosper you and not to harm
you, plans to give you hope and a future."

JEREMIAH 29:11, NIV

It was my senior year in college and I had just joined a new church. After three years of school and drifting from church to church, this was a good and stable change. On my first Sunday I signed up for a Bible study. I was hoping there would be other young adults in the class, but alas, God had other plans. On our first meeting I noticed that most of my study group was much older. They had grown children of their own and even grandchildren!

"So much for like-minded young adults," I thought. As we went around introducing ourselves, it came to my attention that everyone seemed to be living a life of continuity and purpose, yet I was just a college student getting ready to face a future in the "real world." Thankfully, our study took us through Jeremiah 29:11. God has a plan for each and every one of us and He promises a future with hope. I was comforted and the connection was clear that even in the midst of my wandering from church to church or to making important life decisions, God would be there nurturing hope into a life of continuity in Him.

The following year after graduation, I literally read this verse daily, for there were times of uncertainty and hopelessness. Yet even then, and more apparent now as I teach in Brazil, God's still feeding my future with hope.

LIVING OUT GOD'S PLAN FOR MY LIFE

Sometimes we think we know the perfect situation for God to place us in so that we can grow. We may think what we need are people just like ourselves to fellowship with or we may think we need to find some super-hero Christians to mentor us. However, because God knows us better than we know ourselves, He knows exactly what we need, and may surprise us with people who are just the right ones to lead us where He wants us to go.

VANESSA JO CHIPE, www.EditorialCoffee.com

WHAT I LEARNED FROM GOD TODAY...

Fear of Pain

"Do not fear therefore;
you are of more value than many sparrows."

MATTHEW 10:31

This surely has to be something from the script of an old movie, I thought. The unexpected phone call from a doctor telling me that I had a quickly spreading cancer seemed unreal. But it wasn't a movie. It was me, standing in the middle of the kitchen expecting my husband home shortly, and having to teach Bible study in two hours with a death sentence hanging over my head. It is true that one phone call can change your life.

Thus began a journey of praying for a healing while waiting on Him for the next step in my treatment. Walking with God for many years, I knew to cast my cares upon Him. What did become a burden was the heartache I was giving to those who loved me.

If He had given me the choice, I would not have chosen to go home now. However, by grace, I was able to trust Him if that was His will. Fear hit me big time concerning the pain I was convinced I would have to endure. I had never been one who was able to even go to sleep with the slightest pain. Dying I could handle—pain I couldn't.

God did heal me, and delivered me in a special way

from my deep fear of pain. In some ways that means even more to me than the physical healing He also sent.

LIVING OUT GOD'S PLAN FOR MY LIFE
While not everyone has to deal with pain, it is a daily part of life for many. But God is faithful to us in the middle of our circumstances—whatever they are.

FRAN FERNANDEZ, www.EditorialCoffee.com

WHAT I LEARNED FROM GOD TODAY...

A Thank-You Note for Dad

*We give thanks to the God
and Father of our Lord Jesus Christ,
praying always for you....*

COLOSSIANS 1:3

Dear Dad,

Do you remember our vacation when I was ten? That was the year we went to a dude ranch in Texas. What an adventure for a kid! There were trail rides, hayrides, and donkey-drawn cart rides. We swam in moss-shaded riverbed. And who could forget the tantalizing Texas barbecues over smoky campfires?

But what I remember most was the night I asked you to hear my prayers before going to bed. You always listened to my prayers. It was our bedtime ritual. But one night was different from any other. It marked a new chapter in my life.

You told me I should say my prayers alone to my Heavenly Father. "After all," you said, "your daddy won't always be here to listen to your prayers."

Did you know I cried myself to sleep that night? The realization that my daddy would not "always be there" ripped through my heart like a searing bolt of lightning. Salty tears dampened my pillow.

A little more than a decade later my pillow was again wet

with tears. This time the truth of that realization had become reality. As I cried out to my Heavenly Father, He comforted me with the assurance that you were now in His presence.

How thankful I am that you showed me the way so many years before. My Heavenly Father is always there to listen to my prayers. And I thank Him often for you.

LIVING OUT GOD'S PLAN FOR MY LIFE
Then you will call upon Me and go
and pray to Me, and I will listen to you.

JEREMIAH 29:12

SHARI PHILMECK, www.EditorialCoffee.com

WHAT I LEARNED FROM GOD TODAY...

Thank God in Advance

And my God shall supply all your need
according to His riches in glory by Christ Jesus.

PHILIPPIANS 4:19

Positive confession is a powerful force in the life of a believer. This does not mean talking boastfully or claiming God's deliverance apart from His expressed will for your life. Thanking God for His faithfulness and provision is an indication of your submission to His will regardless of your hopes or expectations. Seasons of life may not turn out the way you thought. You may struggle. Mary and Martha watched as their brother died. However, because we serve a risen Lord and Savior, we know that no matter what we face in this life, God will ultimately deliver us from all evil. He will bless us as we seek to know Him intimately. He will guard, protect, and lead us into a place of great blessing and hope.

LIVING OUT GOD'S PLAN FOR MY LIFE

Have you trusted the Savior with your unmet needs, or are you still focused on satisfying your hopes and desires as quickly as possible? Only God can completely meet your needs. Trust Him—give Him your burden to carry and you will witness a tremendous miracle.

DR. CHARLES STANLEY, *Living the Extraordinary Life*

WHAT I LEARNED FROM GOD TODAY...

ACKNOWLEDGMENTS

The Dehydrated Heart by Max Lucado, from *Come Thirsty*, copyright © 2004 by Max Lucado, W Publishing Group, pp. 11–12, 16. Used by permission.

Epiphanies by Naomi Judd, from *The Transparent Life*, copyright © 2005 by Naomi Judd, J. Countryman, pp. 14–15. Used by permission.

Everyone Wants to Know the Secret by Hank Hanegraaff, from T*he Bible Answer Book*, copyright © 2004 by Hank Hanegraaff, J. Countryman, pp. 49–50. Used by permission.

God Listens by Eugene H. Peterson, from *A Message of Comfort and Hope*, copyright © 2005 by Eugene H. Peterson, J. Countryman, pp. 13–18. Used by permission of NavPress, Colorado Springs, CO. All rights reserved.

What If? by Franklin Graham with Ross Rhoads, from *All for Jesus*, copyright © 2003, Nelson Books, pp. 17–18. Used by permission.

A Place to Heal by Terri Blackstock, from *The Gifted*, copyright © 2002 by Terri Blackstock, W Publishing Group, pp. ix–x. Used by permission.

The Cross Is Not in the Cellar by Sheila Walsh, from *Come As You Are*, copyright © 2005 by Sheila Walsh, J. Countryman, pp. 121–122. Used by permission.

Sin Is the Monster We Love to Deny by Frank Peretti, from *The Oath*, copyright © 1995, 2003 by Frank Peretti, Westbow Press, pp. ix–x. Used by permission.

Walk into Your Future by Paula White, from *A Sensational Life*, copyright © 2005 by Paula White, J. Countryman, pp. 16–19. Used by permission.

His Presence Is Sure by Dr. Charles Stanley, *Living the Extraordinary Life,* copyright © 2005 by Charles Stanley, Nelson Books, p. 44. Used by permission.